Ruth and Charlie in Love and War, 1941-1945

Ruth and Charlie
in
Love and War, 1941–1945

BY
JAMES L. DAVIS
RESEARCHED AND EDITED
BY
RACHEL DAVIS

SANTA FE

Sunstone books may be purchased for educational, business, or sales promotional use.
For information please write: Special Markets Department, Sunstone Press,
P.O. Box 2321, Santa Fe, New Mexico 87504-2321.
Printed on acid-free paper
♾
eBook: 978-1-61139-792-5

Library of Congress Cataloging-in-Publication Data

Names: Davis, Charles, Edwin, 1922- author | Bachschmid, Ruth author | Davis, James, L., 1940- compiler | Davis, Rachel (daughter of James L. Davis) compiler
Title: Ruth and Charlie in love and war, 1941-1945 / James L Davis ; researched and edited by Rachel Davis.
Description: Santa Fe : Sunstone Press, [2026] | Summary: "Summaries of letters between Charles Edwin Davis and Ruth Bachschmid during World War
II"-- Provided by publisher.
Identifiers: LCCN 2026006715 | ISBN 9781632937865 paperback
Subjects: LCSH: Davis, Charles, Edwin, 1922- | Bachschmid, Ruth | United States. Army Air Forces | World War, 1939-1945--United States | World War, 1939-1945 | Soldiers--United States | LCGFT: Autobiographies | Personal correspondence | Biographies | Personal narratives
Classification: LCC D790.2 .D37 2026 | DDC 940.548173--dc23/eng/20260212
LC record available at https://lccn.loc.gov/2026006715

WWW.SUNSTONEPRESS.COM
SUNSTONE PRESS / POST OFFICE BOX 2321 / SANTA FE, NM 87504-2321 /USA
(505) 988-4418

CONTENTS

A 6-cent air mail stamp impression.

A humorous postcard his mother sent to Charlie.

INTRODUCTION

It was a different time, a difficult time. War had been raging in Europe for two years without United States participation, and U.S. isolationists were striving to keep it that way. But the Japanese attack on Pearl Harbor, Hawaii, on December 7, 1941, would change that. U.S. soldiers and sailors would be sent to fight the German Axis in Europe and the Japanese in Asia and the South Pacific. World War II would be in full blast for four years.

I lived through that period, but only as a small child. The situation was quite different for my brother, Charles Edwin Davis, who was known by most people as Charlie and who signed his love letters as Chas. He was 18 when I was born on October 28, 1940. Our mother, Ada Virginia Davis, was 40, and our father, Ross Davis, was 42. Mom always referred to me as her "Surprise Baby."

Young Charlie holds baby Jimmie.

The Bachschmid girls, Helen (l) and Ruth about 1923.

Our parents and Charlie lived in Grand Prairie, Texas, near Dallas, for many years. But they moved to Austin in the late 1930s so Ross could find work. That move proved eventful for Charlie, for it was in Austin that he met and became romantically involved with Ruth Bachschmid. She was a real beauty who lived in Austin with her mother, Lena Bachschmid, older sister Helen and younger brother Arnold, who was known to family and friends as Sonny. Lena's husband and the three children's father, Emil Bachschmid, died in 1934 at Caldwell, Texas. Both Lena and Emil were German immigrants. Their children were born in the U.S. and, thus, automatically were American citizens.

Ruth and Charlie had been dating for two years when a Davis family crisis occurred in the fall of 1941. Ross was diagnosed with incurable cancer, and he wanted to die in his hometown of Grand Prairie. Mother and Charlie made a quick decision to take Ross and the infant me and grant his wish. That move initiated a four-year period of letter-writing between Ruth and Charlie that totaled several hundred letters. Ross died on January 23, 1942. Shortly afterward Mother picked me up and moved back to Austin. There, with $4,000 from Ross's life insurance policy, she bought a house in West Austin and divided it into rented rooms and an apartment. The house at 507 Oakland Avenue provided us with a comfortable home and income until I graduated from the University of Texas with journalism and government degrees in 1964 and left Austin to work as a journalist. Mother lived there until she died in 1981. The house later was razed for construction of a two-story office building.

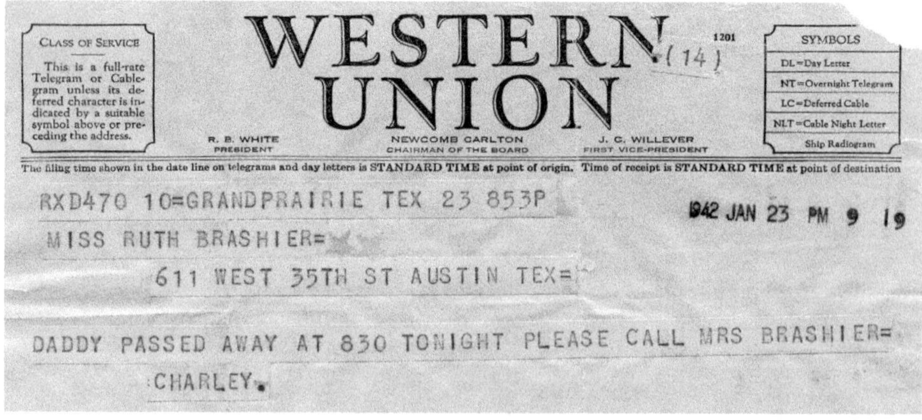

WESTERN UNION

CLASS OF SERVICE
This is a full-rate Telegram or Cablegram unless its deferred character is indicated by a suitable symbol above or preceding the address.

R. B. WHITE, PRESIDENT — NEWCOMB CARLTON, CHAIRMAN OF THE BOARD — J. C. WILLEVER, FIRST VICE-PRESIDENT

1201 (14)

SYMBOLS
DL=Day Letter
NT=Overnight Telegram
LC=Deferred Cable
NLT=Cable Night Letter
Ship Radiogram

The filing time shown in the date line on telegrams and day letters is STANDARD TIME at point of origin. Time of receipt is STANDARD TIME at point of destination

RXD470 10=GRANDPRAIRIE TEX 23 853P — 1942 JAN 23 PM 9 19

MISS RUTH BRASHIER=

611 WEST 35TH ST AUSTIN TEX=

DADDY PASSED AWAY AT 830 TONIGHT PLEASE CALL MRS BRASHIER=

CHARLEY.

One of several telegrams Charlie sent to family and friends about his father's death.

Charlie and Ruth in a Thorndale, Texas park.

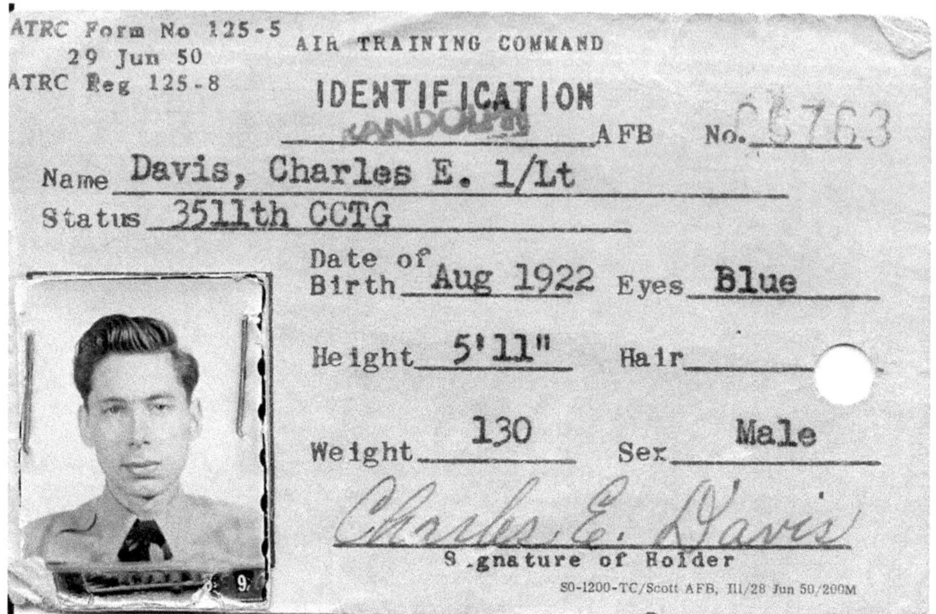

ATRC Form No 125-5
29 Jun 50
ATRC Reg 125-8

AIR TRAINING COMMAND

IDENTIFICATION

AFB No.

Name Davis, Charles E. 1/Lt

Status 3511th CCTG

Date of Birth Aug 1922 Eyes Blue

Height 5'11" Hair

Weight 130 Sex Male

Charles E. Davis

Signature of Holder

S0-1200-TC/Scott AFB, Ill/28 Jun 50/200M

Charlie's Air Training ID Card.

After Ross died, Charlie elected to stay in Grand Prairie, much to Ruth's dismay. He took a job with Douglas Aircraft Company which was making airplanes for the U.S. Military. He tried to maintain a relationship with Ruth through occasional letters, weekend phone calls and occasional 400-mile round trips to see her. But none of that was enough for Ruth. She constantly wrote letters urging him to "come down." Ruth was two years older than Charlie and her letters indicate she was interested in marriage. Perhaps Charlie's decision to stay in Grand Prairie indicated he was not as anxious to marry as she was, at least at that time. He was only nineteen.

Ruth wrote to him frequently. She obviously tried to make him jealous by mentioning her dates and relationships with other men, a tactic that didn't always work well. Most of the letters between them expressed great love, but some were bitter and biting. I inherited many of the letters, about 400, but that's not all of them. I have only letters from Ruth to Charlie when he was in Grand Prairie or at military bases in the U.S. I have mostly letters from him to her after he was sent overseas and flew cargo planes from island to island in the South Pacific. But I know that they were writing to each other the entire time they were apart because the letters that I have frequently refer to questions or information mentioned in letters they had received. And later letters indicate at some point they agreed to write to each other every day that he was away.

My daughter, Rachel Davis, and I spent many hours reading the letters I have, selecting and summarizing the most interesting ones and putting them in chronological order. We found that Ruth's letters generally were well written, with few grammatical errors. The same cannot be said of Charlie's letters. They suffer from frequent grammatical errors, such as putting commas between sentences instead of periods. We corrected some problems to clarify what he meant to say. Others we left to show readers his way of writing. Both lovers consistently used "cause" to mean "because." Since we summarized the selected letters, we used three dots such as ... to indicate there were uninteresting sections that we eliminated. Their letters frequently are quite long, so we felt that summarizing many of them was better than running a few in full.

So let's get to the selected letter summaries.

Two-person Bi-planes used for flight training.

1941

This was a significant year for Ruth and Charlie. Their two-year, in-person love affair suddenly was interrupted and their letter-writing connection began. And, of course, World War II affected practically everyone.

11/17/41

The first letter of the series came to Ruth in Austin, Texas, from Charlie confirming that he was in Grand Prairie, Texas, to be with his dying father, which he had told her in an earlier phone call seemed likely. She was not happy, and she fired off a special delivery letter back. He had expressed regret that he had to move away from her.

She replied: "Talk about feeling awful. I just knew that you had let me down. You don't have to tell me how lonesome you feel because I feel the same. After you called me Saturday, and I realized that you were going, I almost went nuts. I almost called you to beg you not to go." ... She later switched to a more positive reaction. She expressed hope that he soon would find work in the Grand Prairie area, adding: "Now, regardless of what happens and how awful you feel you are going to stick it out so don't let it get you down."

11/20/41

Ruth was at work when her sister Helen called and said that a special delivery letter from Charlie had come to their house. Ruth told Helen to read it to her. The big news in the letter was that he had landed a job at Douglas Aircraft near Dallas, which was already producing war planes under the assumption that the

United States either would be at war soon or would provide help to friendly nations already at war. Ruth worked at the Western Auto store in downtown Austin and wrote back that she was going to a party for employees that evening.

11/24/41

Ruth was feeling low and urged Charlie to "come down" for the weekend. That was a common plea in her letters, frequently with a touch of humor. This time she wrote: "If you don't come down this weekend I shall never forgive you. On top of that, I'll sue you for neglect and desertion."

12/3/41

Ruth learned from a letter from Charlie in Grand Prairie that I was in a local hospital with pneumonia. "So sorry Jimmy is sick and hopefully feeling OK again," she wrote. She referred to me as "Jimmy," although my mother always spelled my name as 'Jimmie." I often wished later that Ruth's way had won. Mother's spelling got me into fights with other boys who teased me about having a girl's name.

12/4/41

Ruth sometimes wrote with a touch of biting humor about being jealous of Charlie being with other women. This time she wrote: "This is the third letter this week. Don't think for a moment that I intend to let B______ (a young woman interested in Charlie) get ahead of me. Here's hoping she doesn't still write two a day cause I can't keep up with that rate." In an example of her sharp humor, she closed with: "Love (or should I say as always?) Ruth."

12/6/41

In another letter, Ruth said she was "pooped out" from Christmas shopping in a town "swamped with shoppers and football fans. I saw your two girlfriends, H______ and F_______, but I didn't go out of my way to speak to them."

12/8/41

On the day after the Japanese attacked Pearl Harbor, Ruth wrote asking Charlie what he thought about "the war situation." On a personal note, she predicted that Charlie would not be drafted as long as he was doing "defense work" at Douglas Aircraft Company. "I hate to call Minnie this morning cause I just know Newton won't get to come home for X-mas now. Poor kid, I just know she's heartbroken cause she had made so many plans. Helen is scared to death too cause Al is a reserve officer and can be called on 24 hours notice. You don't suppose this will spoil our weekends, do you?"

Minnie was a good friend of Ruth's who was dating Newton. Helen was Ruth's sister who dated and ultimately married Al Price.

12/16/41

Ruth frequently teased Charlie with stories about other men chasing her, probably in an attempt to make him jealous. In this letter she identified a married man who was pursuing her, but I have disguised the names of him and his wife to protect the innocent—and the guilty. Ruth's letter said: "X_______'s wife left for California, and he has invited me to spend the evening quietly at home ... I am having an awful time resisting him, but since Mrs. X_______ is the female wrestler type, I have decided to pass up this splendid offer."

The use of humor to make a point was one of Ruth's talents.

U.S. POSTAGE
6¢
VIA AIR MAIL

1942

The first letter we have chosen for 1942 is undated, but Ruth obviously wrote it to Charlie before October of that year because that was the date that he left Douglas Aircraft and joined the Army Air Corps. As you will see, she is concerned about Charlie's future. Surprisingly, she doesn't jump at the chance to have him back to Austin from Grand Prairie. In fact, she apparently—and probably accidently—talked him out of returning to Austin to work for a laundry. Here's the summary of that letter followed by other interesting ones she wrote that year.

Undated 1942

"Wed. evening about 10:30 p.m. (my bedtime): Dearest Charlie, Before I go to bed guess I had better answer the letter I received this morning. I am really, really glad that you are coming back to Austin. You know I am. I've been thinking all day about the swell fun we used to have and how it now can be continued. I have also been thinking along some serious lines and have reached this conclusion: I don't know how much you'll be making at the White Laundry, but I honestly believe that if you're coming back to Austin with the intention of working and getting an education at the same time, no matter how much difference there is in your salary, I still think you will profit in the long run. However, if you're going to fool around and not give a darn about studying like you used to, you might as well stay where you are. I really believe Charlie that you have learned a lot this past year and will try to be more serious minded and studious in the future. Okay—you can swell up and explode now cause I'm through with my little lecture."

She then recommended a "really cute movie" called "My Gal Sal" and detailed her work duties that week before coming back to the moving issue: "When will you move back down? I don't believe you're coming back until everything is completely settled."

Charlie obviously decided to stay in his Douglas Aircraft job until he joined the military in October of 1942.

1/1/42

Ruth said she went to "a super deluxe wonderful movie" that he must see called "Louisiana Purchase." She added: "If you are still wondering how we girls get into our girdles, see this show and watch Bob Hope's demonstration. It's really wonderful cause he goes through every motion step by step."

1/21/42

"I heard the Ink Spots play 'Someone Is Rocking My Dreamboat' this morning and I agree with you. It is very pretty ... The Blackout here was very exciting. I watched it with one eye open and the other closed." She ended the letter with: "Sorry to hear that your daddy is worse. I'm afraid the next few weeks will be real hard for you but you will take it."

1/22/42

Her next letter started with: "Darling, I'm so worried about your daddy. I can't help but think of him all of the time."

1/23/42

Ruth's next letter was written on the day that Ross Davis died of cancer in Grand Prairie: January 23, 1942. It's impossible to know whether she knew of his death before writing this letter, maybe from a phone call, or she just knew that death was coming. Either way, her lead-in to her letter is a bit strange: "I wish you could come down this weekend. But I know it's impossible. I feel bad for your daddy, and I know how awful it must make you feel."

1/26/42

Three days after Ross Davis died Ruth wrote: "I hope you can come down cause two weeks has been too long already." This letter clearly demonstrates how she kept pressing him to make the 200-mile trip to Austin, even under difficult circumstances.

1/30/42

Ruth wrote to Charlie in Grand Prairie: "When I didn't get a letter from you yesterday, I was forced to believe that loneliness had gotten the better of you and you had taken on one of those 35 year old ton weight babies you are always writing about."

That's another example of her humor.

2/18/42

Ruth told Charlie: "I know the things I said to you in that letter were really mean, but I couldn't help it because you hurt my feelings." She never explained what he did to hurt her feelings.

3/24/42

Apparently, there was a disagreement over Ruth's relationship with Lewis, a young man who Ruth dated occasionally while Charlie was in Grand Prairie. Charlie wrote Ruth apologizing "for being wrong about Saturday night." Apparently, the three of them had been together during one of Charlie's trips to Austin. Ruth answered Charlie's apology letter with: "The only way you were wrong was the way you felt about Lewis. You know it wasn't his fault that I acted the way that I did. I am never influenced by others. I act the way I feel like acting."

3/30/42

Minnie was a co-worker of Ruth's at Western Auto and a close friend of both Ruth and Charlie. It's impossible to know how serious Ruth meant this letter to him. My guess is, not very.

“Say, what’s the meaning of all the cooing you and Minnie are handing each other? I’ve always been suspicious of you and her. Better be careful or I’ll name her as correspondent when I get ready to divorce you.”

This, of course, was long before they married, and Ruth and Minnie remained close friends.

4/8/42

“I know another funny joke now,” Ruth said, trying to be funny herself. “It’s about a Negro and a blackout. Naturally I wouldn’t tell you the joke. I just want you to be curious, see?”

Charlie indicated in a letter he sent later from the South Pacific during the war that he was more liberal on racial issues than she was.

5/9/42

“I will be most unhappy if you don’t come down on weekends anymore,” Ruth wrote to Charlie. “Are you sure your hours will be changed?” She was reacting to his news that his employer had changed work hours so it would be more difficult for him to drive to Austin to see her. “North American is beginning to annoy me terribly, and you can tell them I said so,” she added.

I doubt that Charlie said anything to the company. In fact, he might have made up the claim in an effort to get relief from her constant pleas for him to “come down.” And despite his claim about tighter hours, he continued to make occasional trips to Austin to visit with Ruth, Mother and me.

5/32/42

Referring to her younger brother, Ruth’s letter nipped at Charlie about his lack of interest in religion: “Sonny is being confirmed Sunday, (confirmation is something connected with church in case you don’t know)” Then switching subjects, she added: “I read in the paper today that boys between 18 and 20 register on June 30. Guess that means you, no? If you get drafted, I don’t know what I will do.”

As you will see later in Charlie's letters from the South Pacific, he became much more religious in the war zone. Reading his letters reminded me of the saying that there are no atheists in foxholes.

7/18/42

Probably attempting to stir up some jealousy, Ruth wrote to Charlie: "Louis may come in this weekend, unless his folks come to see him. If he does come, I'll tell him you said he should go to h——. Aren't you ashamed? Nice boys don't talk like that ... I still kind of like you best. Don't know why, but I do and can't help it."

8/5/42

Charlie sent Ruth a puppy, which she named Charles Edwin. But she wrote an unusual thank you note: "Hello Sarcastic (I mean Darling Precious): I think the puppy is just too darling. But I can't say as much for the nasty sarcastic note attached. ...You were referring to one particular person, weren't you? I believe we're just about even now."

We can't be certain who that "particular person" was since Ruth dated several men and frequently mentioned them in letters to Charlie. Her attempts to make him jealous frequently backfired.

8/12/42

"Hello Darling. As usual I'm sneaking you a letter. One of these days I'll get caught and then you'll have to support me the rest of my life."

A fair number of Ruth's letters were written on stationary of businesses where she worked, and she sometimes said her writing was possible because the boss had stepped out for some reason. This time the "important" information she needed to convey included: "My favorite song for the moment is 'A Sinner Kissed an Angel.' I think it's just too wicked. I am also crazy about 'He's My Guy 'cause it reminds me of you."

8/13/42

Ruth wrote to Charlie that: "While the boss is away the secretary plays and that's what I am doing right now. What I want to know is are you coming down this weekend? Or not?" She added that in recent letters to her he didn't say much about it. "So I'm still in the dark … I want you to come down. I miss you. Lots of Love, Ruth."

8/16/42

It was Sunday afternoon. Ruth was resting at home listening to the radio.

"Sure heard some great music this afternoon. Do you like 'Idaho'?" she asked in a letter to Charlie, who was still working at Douglas Aircraft. She added: "Saw a swell show last night: 'Wings for The Eagle.' It's a picture made in an airplane factory so be sure to see it."

In October 1942 Charlie resigned from Douglas Aircraft and enlisted in the Army Air Corps. He told Ruth that he could have kept working at building airplanes, but he decided that his real desire was to fly one. Ruth was not happy with his decision because it would take him far away from Austin, but in her letters to him she tried to be supportive.

10/31/42

This letter started off friendly and chatty about having to clean out the garage. Then the letter's tone changed dramatically:

"That little card you sent me was rather on the sarcastic side, wasn't it? Maybe I've been thinking seriously about us lately. Guess I'd better go back to the old way since that seems to be the way you want it. I'm sorry. Guess it's none of my business to try to correct your faults. From now on tell me anything and when I doubt you, I'll just go on wondering if I ever can believe you. I'm not only referring to what you told me since you have been in the Army. I'm just remembering you like I usually do every other month. I've been thinking seriously about us lately. That's why I feel this way."

11/2/42

"I'm still sick at my stomach and sure as heck can't figure out why," Ruth wrote, "Went to a midnight show with A_ _ _. I didn't want to go but he insisted and since he leaves Tuesday I thought I might as well make him happy. Saw 'Night in Manhattan' and it was really boring." She added that her sister, Helen, "has another feather in her cap" because her boyfriend and future husband Al Price had been made a first lieutenant. "I still hold my head up high and insist that a buck private is just as nice, and I have really convinced myself that that is right."

11/6/42

Ruth wrote: "Sweet, Dearest, Darling, Precious Charlie: Gosh you're getting good at sarcastic letters. Guess you learned it from me, though. You usually learn your bad habits from me, don't you?" And she closed with: "Yours Forever Too. Ruth," probably making fun of a closing from a Charlie letter.

11/19/42

"I've always been crazy about you, but I've never felt like this," Ruth wrote. "In other words, in other words, I'm head-over-heels in love and I like it."

11/27/42

Ruth opened this letter with an apology and an accusation: "I'm sorry I acted mean yesterday, but you really did hurt my feelings. Don't try to figure out why because you don't realize what you did. I know you're jealous but you're not half as jealous as I am. I want you all to myself and I don't want you to even halfway act like you like anybody else because I can't stand it. I know that's silly after the way I do you, but you can take things much better than I. You've proved it dozens of times."

12/9/42

Ruth wrote Charlie that her sister Helen was baking cookies to send to her boyfriend, Al Price, but don't expect the same from her. "I'm just not the type," she added.

I can testify that she became that type. After she and Charlie were living in student housing while he attended the University of Texas, she made friends in their neighborhood and took cooking tips. Ruth was good at just about anything she tried, and cooking was no different, even cookies. I especially can testify to that.

12/17/42

"I'm thrilled to death at your prospects of coming home for Christmas. That would be super wonderful," she wrote to Charlie. He did make it home for Christmas and after he returned to his base, she wrote another letter on December 27 saying, "The last three days were wonderful."

But apparently, they weren't perfect, for she added: "I'm sorry you don't understand me."

1943

After Charlie joined the Army Air Corps in October 1942 and completed basic training, he spent most of 1943 moving among various Air Corps bases in the United States due to various training assignments. These ranged from bases at San Antonio and Pecos in Texas to ones in Wisconsin, Oklahoma and Utah. It was during flight training at Pecos that he crashed an airplane and suffered minor injuries. This also was the year that he and Ruth became engaged, but marriage had to wait much longer. Now more letter summaries.

Charlie in his pilot's uniform.

Charlie with crashed plane at Pecos Field Texas. This also was the year that he and Ruth became engaged, but marriage had to wait much longer.

1/1/1943

Ruth wrote Charlie: "Your mother came by the store yesterday and said she had called me about three times since yesterday. She is being nice to me. I guess she got over last weekend."

There is no further information on what happened that weekend that made Ruth surprised that our mother "got over" it. But neither Charlie nor I would have been surprised that there was a possible troublesome issue. Ruth and our mother had frequent tense relationships, which made life unpleasant for him and me.

The next two letter summaries are replies from Ruth to a marriage proposal letter from Charlie. Unfortunately, I don't have my brother's proposal letter, but Ruth's reaction to it is surprising. Read her two letter summaries together, remembering that marriage had been on her mind for quite a while.

Charlie preparing to take off, with a smile.

Ruth and Charlie in cold together at the base.

3/13/1943

Ruth received the proposal letter and immediately wrote back to Charlie at his base in Oklahoma: "I just have time for a note...have to spend my lunch hour at the dentist. .... I'll write you a nice long letter tomorrow in answer to your proposal. Hold your breath now—I might turn you down! I love you dearly, Ruth"

3/14/1943

Surprisingly, Ruth waited 36 hours before writing the following:

"Darling, just got back from seeing 'Somewhere I'll Find You.' Sure was wonderful. Boy! Those kisses that Clark Gable dealt out to Lana Turner were enough to put me under my seat. Didn't put me under my seat, though. My resistance is much too high now..."Then after a few more irrelevant remarks she finally got to the important part: "In answer to your question 'Will you marry me on my furlough?' I will be happy to marry you on your next furlough, So the answer is Yes. I would like it very much to be married in a church (preferably the one down home) with only your family and mine present. The thing that worries me is: When and if, you will get that next furlough..."

Ruth's worries about the time element of the wedding were justified. Getting a furlough for a wedding and a week of honeymooning took Charlie more than a year. The ceremony took place in Austin on June 24, 1944.

I was three and have a vague memory of it.

3/25/1943

Ruth tells Charlie that it is raining and lightning "like the dickens" in Austin. "Sometimes I think I've gotten over missing you and then a day like this comes along and then I know I'll never get over being without you." She added: "Why do you think I was angry on the phone call? You know darn well I've never so long as I have known you been mad at you a single time, because I love you so darn much."

Well, those of us who knew her and/or have read some of her letters know that Ruth was angry at Charlie several times, in fact sometimes fairly often.

4/20/1943

Ruth wrote that she had listened on the radio to Bob Hope's broadcast from Camp Hood, Texas, which was part of the program of entertainers performing for the troops. Now, she wrote, she was listening to Red Skelton. She neatly drew a heart with their initials on the envelope. "You didn't know I was artistic, I betcha," she wrote in the letter.

5/24/43

A postcard from Charlie to Ruth from the army base at Kearns, Utah, where he was assigned for a short time: He wrote that he had sent the photos she wanted but commented "they are awful." Apparently, service at that base wasn't too stressful. He added that "We have spent the whole day in town going to shows and skating. I'm thinking of you."

An undated letter from Ruth to Charlie: "How long do you think it will be before you leave Kearns and where do you expect to be sent? I keep my eyes open for cadets now. I still can't figure out the difference in your old insignia and the new one. A picture would help... Mom always questions me, wants to know if I'm worried about you. I always tell her heck no, but I guess there is very little time you're not on my mind."

7/21/43

A rather biting letter from an angry Ruth: "First thing I want to know, what did you write Helen? She had a little P.S, on her last letter saying: "You just ought to know what Charlie told me. I'm always suspicious, you know, so if you don't want me to think what I'm thinking you had better write and tell about it."

Apparently, what he told Helen wasn't too exciting. Once he told her, Ruth didn't make a big deal about it in later letters.

7/22/43

But a letter from Minnie stirred Ruth's anger. It told Ruth that she had received a letter from Charlie saying he would start flying in about two weeks. An upset Ruth immediately wrote Charlie saying, "I don't like lies to come between us."

Obviously, Charlie hadn't told Ruth about starting to fly, probably to avoid worrying her. She had expressed in several letters that she wished he wouldn't take up flying.

7/28/43

Ruth told Charlie that she had been listening to a radio broadcast by President Franklin Roosevelt. "I had hoped listening to the President's speech he would tell us the war is almost over, but no such luck. I had hopes now that the heel has been kicked off the boot."

That apparently was a reference to Benito Mussolini being kicked out of power and killed in Italy, which has a shape commonly referred to as a boot. Mussolini had been a key ally of Adolph Hitler.

8/12/43

Ruth obviously had modified her fears of Charlie flying. She wrote to him at the military base at Oshkosh, Wisconsin, telling him he "must be making headway on flying. I feel better when you're the pilot, promise me that you will pilot. … It's surprising that you will be leaving Oshkosh so soon. I imagine that when you leave Oshkosh things will really be tough."

She obviously was worried that when he finished his training in Wisconsin he would be sent overseas. She wrote that her sister Helen had similar worries about her new husband, Al Price.

Charlie on patrol with a rifle.

A friend declares Charlie "a rough Texan."

Single-engine trainer at War Eagle Field, Lancaster, California.

Biplanes at Thunderbird Field, Arizona.

9/13/43

Charlie had traveled by bus to San Diego, California, to catch a plane ride to his new assignment overseas. His orders did not say where. He wrote to Ruth: "Darling Wife: I will be leaving this week. I wish I knew where...I sent my clothes home cause I can't take them."

9/13/43

That same day he sent a letter indicating he thought he was leaving but then learned that he was not: "Believe it or not Darling but I got to come back to town again. I tried to send a wire but they closed early. I'll be leaving this week, going by air, where? I wish I knew myself. ... It's hard to realize I'm leaving everything behind I love so much: You. So long Darling. I love you so much. Your loving husband Chas."

9/17/43

Charlie had been flown to his new assignment, which he can describe to Ruth only as "Somewhere in New Guinea." He told her he had five of her letters to him waiting when he got there. He added that he read each one seven times. Referring to a man Ruth had dated before their marriage, Charlie said she could go with him while he was away, adding: "I think I can trust him." He ends with, "You don't have to work unless you want to. Love Chas."

10/3/43

Some Place in New Guinea:

When Charlie arrived overseas, he, like other military personnel, had to observe rules limiting how much information on their sites and duties they could reveal, and they had to submit their correspondences for censorship. The process was particularly difficult for Charlie since he and Ruth had promised to write to each other every day while they were apart. He wrote in this letter about planning to pan for gold in a nearby stream and seeing a movie entitled "Summer Storm." He wrote that movies were shown at his base three times a week.

10/7/43

Somewhere in New Guinea.

"My Darling Wife: Gosh, did I ever have a rough time today, We made that 2,000-mile trip again and I flew almost all the way. I also made my first takeoff, That Big Crate (apparently a C-47 cargo plane) made the VC-78 (the plane he had been training on) seem like a baby, What power! What a ship! ... To make the day complete we got caught in a storm while coming up the Valley and we had to come down to tree top level over the jungle. It finally got so bad we flew up the riverbed a couple of feet off the water so we could see. Your Loving Husband Chas."

10/22/43

Ruth wrote to Charlie: "I'm going skating with S. & J. & Minnie." She reported that Al had written to Helen that he was assigned to escort movie star Ginger Rogers to the Officers' Club where he was stationed, but her mother went too. Ruth told about going drinking with Minnie and Lewis. "Minnie and Lewis drank a pint of rum and Minnie spilled a drink on her lap," Ruth wrote. This information about them getting drunk on hard liquor did not sit well with Charlie. He wrote and scolded her about it.

12/8/43

Some Place in New Guinea:

"Claude had arranged dates with nurses," Charlie confessed, "but they had to work." Apparently. Ruth had written to him previously about her problems with our mother. In this letter he mentioned a soldier whose wife liked his family. "Sorry I can't say the same right now. I hope it's better soon."

He added that it would be six months before he could get a leave long enough for him to visit her in Austin.

12/23/43

"Sure wish I had my honey here to fix my old clothes for me," Charlie wrote. "All the buttons are off, sox have holes, shorts no bottom. I'm bad off in general." He also complained that he had been 10 days without a letter from her, adding "How about some pictures of you in shorts? That new figure of yours would look sweet in shorts and could help my morale. Really, you can let me see you in shorts now that we are married. Love Chas"

In another letter Charlie wrote that he was sorry he had not earlier given Ruth his car, which was in a garage near our mother's house. "What I wanted was both of you to share it, but I guess that was wishful thinking."

Ruth and our mother often had a tense relationship. I know that Mom wanted to keep the car even though she didn't drive. Charlie eventually got in the middle of the dispute and gave control of the car to Ruth. Mother was NOT happy.

Charlie and friends out on a hike.

Charlie (standing on the left) poses with friends.

1944

At the start of this year, Charlie still was "Somewhere in New Guinea," unable to be more specific due to censorship restrictions. Unfortunately, my collection of letters is sparce for the first nine months of 1944. The main reason for that was that Charlie received a leave so he could return to Texas and marry Ruth. The wedding took place in Austin on June 29, 1944, and they had a short honeymoon in Pecos. Then Charlie remained at the Pecos airfield for about two months while awaiting orders on where he should go. He was hoping for Europe, but the Army sent him back to the South Pacific. Now we pick up where my 1994 letter summaries start.

After Ruth returned home alone, she wrote several letters to Charlie while he was awaiting orders at Pecos. Two of them concerned her practicing to drive their car so she could drive to Pecos when Charlie wasn't tied up with work. Two others described wedding gifts they received, plus in one she told him he was too thin and needed to gain some weight.

10/7/44

Somewhere in New Guinea.

"To my very sweet wife: I'm one pleased 2nd Lt. tonight for I spent the whole day flying as 1st Pilot. I've got that old feeling again for I'm not one little bit scared to fly this ship. Flying is fun again now. ... I went to a P.X. in another town today and bought $3 worth of candy, mints and gum. ... We have our little house fixed up real swell now, it's got that homely appearance now. It's costing me $18.50 to live over here each month so will send you extra money each month."

10/8/44

Somewhere in New Guinea.

"I had a swell time at the beach today, the waves were so high I was afraid to go out to (sic) far. The water here is so warm. Our (unclear) Club had a meeting tonight and pooled all the liquor we could find, which in turn we are going to trade for an ice box. They brought in everything from rubbing alcohol on up. I was told today that all of us would probably be made 1st Lt. in six months which won't make me one bit mad. I kinda had hoped of getting back in a year or so but I'm afraid now I'll have to see the whole thing through."

10/10/44

New Guinea

Charlie told Ruth that he had received five letters from her, and that it made him "so happy I could almost cry ... If you would like to go out with E_______ I won't care too much, guess I can trust him cause he's rather old. ... Darling what about once a week write me a rather gooey love letter cause once a week will help my morale a lot."

10/12/44

"I won't be able to write very much cause I have flown two days and still have to fly tomorrow, darn it. We made a trip yesterday and had to land at another place. I had to sleep in a dugout affair. I only had one meal in 36 hours. Some fun. I saw my first Jap today. We flew real low over a certain place and I saw them dash into the bushes. I also waved at the headhunters in a village, bet they were wishing we'd fall so they could have us for supper. ... Remind me to tell you about this certain trip when I come home. I love you precious, love you very much. Love Chas."

Obviously, Charlie was afraid that writing about "this certain trip" would not make it past a censor.

10/12/44

Letter No. 2. He forgot to mention something in letter No. 1 that day: "I didn't file any income tax last year. Do what you want about it." He added that a G.I. offered him $150 for his .45 pistol. He said he was tempted but he had seen jungle that would take months to walk out of if they had to land. And he figured he would need that pistol. "P.S. Sweet I'm going trade me a bottle of liquor for a little native girl. Get me one that's young and bring her up the way I want her. The fellows say after a few months these black girls look white to a person, you know."

Then he ended with "Har Har" to let Ruth know that he was joking.

10/14/44

"I just finished signing my pay voucher and I will send you four hundred dollars the 30th of Oct. by money order. I've spent about 6 dollars since I arrived here, mostly for stuff at the P.X., so you can see I live very cheap. ... Darling I hope my letters aren't to (sic) boring. I could really write some humdingers if I could tell you what I do, but that's impossible. Love Chas."

Somehow Charlie got mixed up on the dates and put the same one on two letters:

10/15/44

New Guinea.

"My Sweet Darling: I really been doing some tall flying the past couple of days. Since I checked out in a 47 I have had to do almost all the flying. I really had a scare yesterday for my co-pilot took over the controls long enough to start dogfighting with a P-38. Those (C-47s) are good planes, but I don't care to put them beyond their limits. The bad part about these trips is I often miss 2 meals a day. ... The jungle gets more guys down here than the Japs do. This is a hell of a place to have to fight a war. Darling, get yourself a good map of New Guinea and you can almost tell where I've been."

10/15/44

"I made myself a little fishing line today and followed a small stream up into the jungle but guess there were no fish in it. It ends with my falling into the water and going swimming. … I have already flown over 15 missions and I've really built my time up a lot, in the near future I will be getting a lot of combat time. Seems funny to be going after Japs without guns. … P.S. I'm (with) a new bunch of fellows. I haven't the slightest idea where the others went. Darling you will have to do some between the lines reading in my letters." In a separate letter he reminisced about how the rain reminded him "of those rainy nights we spent in our little room in dear old Pecos" after their wedding. "P.S. We're having a big beer party tomorrow night."

10/16/44

"Rainy Night in New Guinea." After some small talk about letters, Charlie wrote to Ruth about a serious matter: "I filed an income tax for 1941 through 42 in Oklahoma but not for 43 or 44. I guess I'll be going to jail after the war." …That was his only comment about taxes. Answering a question from Ruth about what to do with some extra savings they had, he wrote, "I suggest you put the money in Postal Savings but you decide."

10/17/44

"My Darling Wife: Gosh do I feel punk this morning, for that beer party nearly got me down," he confessed. "We had a jolly good time of it, sang songs, shot craps, played blackjack. I had to make several trips to the jungle during the morning hours. … I've been listening to Tokyo Radio. Tokyo Rose is going strong, telling how we've lost the war."

He also complained how the water there has turned his teeth a dull brown.

10/19/44

"My Darling Ruth: It really was swell coming in from a long trip and finding a very sweet letter from a very sweet person. I do hate to make long missions for I always have to sleep in someone else's bed and can't clean up until I return. …

This will probably be a very calm Xmas for me for I will probably fly that day. Funny how nothing seems to matter anymore. I just live for the day till I come home to you."

10/19/44

New Guinea.

"Here comes my second letter for today ... Writing you makes everything seem better." He added that he just received two letters from Ruth that "make me feel 100 % better to know everything is ok in the Davis family. Gee it is just a sweet family like my three that makes it worth all the hell we go through over here. ... So old Jim boy will be four next week, gee he's growing up and I don't even realize it. Guess I will have to have one of our own someday."

10/20/44

New Guinea.

"My Darling Wife: Being I have to spend the night away from home, I decided to write you before I took off, it's still dark outside and raining at that." He asked her to send his camera and a hunting knife to him. "Send me a nice hunting knife. Get one that (has) got a large blade and pretty handle, A man over here is judged by the knife he has."

10/21/44

Charlie wrote two letters with this date, The first one just explained why he couldn't write much. He had to get up at three a.m. to fly a mission. The second one opened by saying he got back from the mission and "made a bee line for the Mess Hall. It was a long mission, and I had gone 36 hours without eating." Apparently replying to a question from Ruth, he said: "I'm in 5th Air Force." Reacting to news from her, he wrote: 'So my little wife is a working girl now." He ended with a story about getting caught in a storm and having to land at an abandoned Japanese airfield. "I sure was glad they weren't there to welcome us."

10/22/44

Charlie wrote to Ruth that he was writing this letter from a plane at 12,000 feet and cooking on an electric stove. "I made toast, veg. soup, tea, cheese and bread," he said, adding: It's really hard to boil water at that height." Then he wrote something he surely knew would please Ruth: "Seeing the valley with its high mountain peaks on each side and the dark rain clouds rushing to meet us made me think of the Bible Scripture: 'Ye though I fly through the Valley of Death, I shall fear no evil, for thou are with me forever.'" Then he added: "I slipped getting out of the plane and wrenched my back."

10/25/44

"Somewhere else. I'm sorry I had to neglect you on letters (the) past few days but I have been so darn busy. I'm on Detach Service for a week so you see I am not at home. I don't like it here very well cause we have bad tents, no beds and poorer food. ... I received five letters last nite, they were written Oct. 1, 2, 3, and 4th, I guess that brings you up to date, up to 11th Oct.,"That was an attempt at humor, and he listed only four dates for five letters. He continued: "I really like the pictures, it seems that my wife gets prettier each day that passes. ... I did some night flying last night for the first time, didn't like it, period."

10/26/44

He had a bad sunburn.

"Never again will I stay in the sun that long ... I went to the show last night and saw Frankie boy in 'Step Lively' ... Most of the pilots went to Austin for training, we really talk over the old hangouts. Honey I know my letters are so dull but it's so hard to write cause there is so little that I can tell you."

Censors checked all outgoing mail to make sure no secret information was included. Charlie obviously did a good job of avoiding censor problems. Only twice did we see where things had been cut out of his letters.

10/29/44

Charlie said he and friends were swimming at the beach.

"The funny part is we (were) standing on the beach and along comes a WAAC in a jeep. She just looked us over and drove on. Some Gal. We're going down to the creek and cool off some beer. I've got to where I really like beer."

10/29/44

"Hello Darling: This is one hot Sunday, it's hot enough to fry eggs on our tent floor ... We are going back home tomorrow (our shack). When I get home (Austin) we are going on some fishing and camping trips that won't wait. I just want to be alone with you. Got to go but I love you precious, love you with all my heart. Love Chas."

10/19/44

New Guinea.

"My Darling Wife: "Gosh, am I glad to get back to my little old house. I did have a nice time while I was gone, for I went swimming every day." ... He wrote that he "will be over here a long time," and added "As soon as we get into combat, I will have a good chance of getting the Air Medal and couple (of) clusters."

10/31/44

New Guinea.

"To the Sweetest Little Wife in the World: I really did think about you on the 29th, gal, I'm an old married man of four months. I remember that little hotel room with the big bath and ceiling fan and me with my sweet little wife ... I wish you could see your hubby play Bridge and Rummy, we have a big game here every night. I guess the news sounds real well now, it even sounds better to me cause I'm having a part in making it."

11/18/44

Netherland East Indies. Charlie's unit was moved temporarily to the Netherland East Indies, which is now Indonesia.

"Dear Little Wife: Gosh, we really had the excitement tonight. A bomb dump near us caught fire and (a) couple blew up. I nearly broke my neck hitting the floor. I went swimming this evening and as usual I cut my big toe but had lots of fun ... Not doing much flying this month. I was getting tired of flying every day."

11/24/44

"My Darling Wife: Gee, what I wouldn't give for just one letter from my wife. It has been 2 weeks since I last had a letter of any sort. Ever since we moved it has been that way. ... Heard a good rumor today, if it's so I'll get a 30 day leave to come home in 10 more months. Sure hope it's so." It wasn't.

11/28/44

Charlie began this letter with an excited report about getting a case of fruit cocktail. He mentioned a poem he had written but didn't give details. He then turned very serious and wrote a second sheet saying:

"I just reread my letter to you and realized just how little I have said. Darling please don't be angry with me for not writing more details and telling how lonesome I am. I get so despondent at times I nearly die. If I ever let myself get into that kind of mood while I'm writing, I'd make you unhappy with words. You mean all the world to me. ... Be sweet and love me till it hurts, cause it (is) hurting me more each day I am away."

11/29/44

Charlie complained about the heat and flies at the base in the Netherland East Indies, but he was happy that he had received more fruit cocktail.

He added: "I had the most foolish thing happen to me yesterday with a new guy who had just been checked out, who used to be a fighter pilot."

It seems that he was flying a plane that Charlie oversaw when he decided to buzz a Japanese airstrip. Charlie was upset because he thought the action was dangerous and needless since "This strip doesn't have any planes."

12/1/44

Charlie's unit had been moved to another area of the Netherland East Indies, and he was not happy.

"It's much nicer where we used to be," he wrote in a letter to Ruth. But, of course, he couldn't say anything that would identify either base's location. "I have neglected to write the last few days but it was due to almost constant flying. … Darling a lot of the stories you hear about this place are rather large, a guy just has to be on his guard and he can get through this deal with all his hair and still sane. The stuff we take for fever makes a person yellow as gold. I'm getting a good suntan to hide my yellow color."

12/6/44

"Same Place. Hello Honey Bet I'm really a long ways back in your doghouse for not writing this week, but my excuse is there's a war going on and it's rough all over. I haven't heard from mother or you in a week now, the mail is still screwed up. … I guess you'll have the Christmas tree up by now. Gosh it would be so much fun if I could help decorate it, that's half the fun of X-mas." He asked her to "buy Mom's and Jim's presents for me, get something they can wear." He added: "Darling please spend part of X-mas with my family for you can take my place for me. Do that for me please."

12/7/44

"Hello Dearest Darling: Gosh Sweet did I feel awful today for I spent the night with Claude and they had a big party at their club. I drank 6 Tom Collins and Claude had to put me to bed, I promise Sweet that will never happen again for I was never so sick in my life."

Ruth had written to Charlie about a man they knew getting out of the military, "It doesn't seem right for a guy to do like that when other guys are going through hell," Charlie said.

12/10/44

Before the war Charlie was not particularly religious, much to Ruth's concern. That changed in the South Pacific. "This makes two Sundays in a row that I've had to fly (and) miss church." He wrote. "I don't know what's come over me but I don't ever want to miss going to church if I can help it." These words surely made Ruth happy.

12/15/44

"Twelve Thousand Feet over Pacific: Here I sit way up here in the blue trying to compose your letter and also keep an eye open for any stray jap planes, some fun. ... We had a big storm last nite and the spray from the ocean was rough. I slept in a puddle of water all night. We have our shack built about 100 feet from the ocean and all we have to do to go swimming is to run and jump in. ... Seems like I'm going to have to land this crate so will have to say bye now. Love Chas."

12/17/44

"Here I am back home to my little shack, these long trips are really rough. Received two of your letters dated Nov. 24th and 21st, which means it took them 26 days to reach me."

12/18/44 Netherland East Indies

"Sweet I'm sorry for all thoughs (sic) sharp cracks I made when we had all those little sore spats we had. I knew what lay ahead of me and I just couldn't help myself. Let's promise never to let it happen again no matter what comes up. Two of the boys who came over with me were killed a month after we got here, they were the few sent to the B-24s, I guess I'm still a lucky fellow as I was sent to this deal (flying cargo and wounded soldiers over relatively safe routes) instead of B-24s." (Bombers flying into dangerous combat).

12/19/44

Charlie apologized to Ruth for not writing to her as often as they had agreed on. His excuse was that he had been "so darn busy." As a wise example, he wrote that he had spent a lot of time reading "The Robe." a best-selling book about the crucifixion of Christ—which she had recommended.

12/21/44

Charlie wrote that he wouldn't be able to send her as much money as previously because he "may go on leave in a couple of months and I'll need the money." He continued: "I really had a good laugh a few minutes ago. Four of us were taking a shower and the Red Cross girls drove up in a jeep and we did (not) see them till it was too late. They seem(ed) to enjoy the show so we kept on showering."

12/23/44

Over the blue Pacific.

"Hello Honey: Just finished showing Hanchey your picture and he said he now understands why I'm so eager to come home." ... Charlie said he and Hanchey were two goof-offs. "We're really a pair us two." Earlier they had eaten a meal with "some Navy boys and what a meal it was, it's a shame (there's) so much difference in the two branches of service."

12/25/44

Over the Pacific.

"I told you I would spend X-mas day in the air, rough war isn't it. I'm sure we will get to eat Christmas dinner cause we intend to find something wrong with the plane about that time." He wrote that there had been a big party the previous night, and he drank only one beer "for I had a feeling of peace and goodwill, and I didn't want to ruin it." Later he lay on a cot and listened to carols while thinking about home and Ruth. "I was happy but the tears just slipped out." He closed with: "You'll probably think I'm nuts but when you are up there in the blue you can imagine you hear the most beautiful singing, just think about a song and the hum of the engine just makes music. Yes I am OK. Love Chas."

12/26/44

In this letter Charlie praised photos of Ruth. "You look so darn cute," he wrote. He hit a more serious tone when he described seeing a Japanese submarine successfully torpedo an American ship. "Poor guys" he said. Then he closed with the news that he had been approved to go on leave sometime around February 20, 1945. "I could sure use that leave," Charlie said, "cause I'm ready for some steak and eggs."

1945

1/7/45

This letter displays the difference between Ruth and Charlie on racial issues.

Charlie wrote: "I have just read the most fascinating book I've ever read, It's kind of on the rough side but it says a lot of real stuff about the slave days in the South, If you care to read a book you will call trash I'll give you the title," which he finally did.

The book was "Strange Fruit" by Lillian Smith, which dealt with the controversial theme of interracial romance. We don't know how Ruth reacted to this letter, but she probably didn't like it, and I would bet that she never read the book.

1/9/45

This is a short note from Charlie saying he has been working all day on the rough house he and his friends are building at their new base in Netherland East Indies. "I'm so tired I can barely stand up … I will write you more tonight." Apparently, he was so tired that he dropped his usual "Love Chas" and instead wrote "Your Loving Hubby Charles."

1/9/45

Charlie wrote Ruth: "Boy have I been lucky. I've had two tires blow out on me just after I have land(ed) this past two weeks … I had a shuttle run today (to) pick up personnel and fly them between islands, some fun."

1/10/45

He was sitting in the doorway of his shack, he told Ruth, "looking at the deep blue Pacific spreading out for thousands of miles, I also marvel at the large cumulus clouds that build up over the water...If I could forget there's a war, it's someplace else I could appreciate all its beauty, but it so happens I can't care for this part of the world, Give me Texas. Your loving one Chas."

1/16/45

He said a letter from Ruth today was the was the first of the week, then he added:

"For the past week I've been on a combat mission up north where it's really rough, I just got back tonight now that it's over I'm so nervous I can hardly write."

He describes living with the crew for a week in the plane without being able to even change clothes. He said upon getting back he found "a whole pile of letters from my honey."

But then his letter turned darker. Obviously, Ruth had questioned his plan to go to Australia on his upcoming leave rather than trying to make a quick trip home.

"I did get kind of teed off about the letter of Dec. 31 giving me hell about my leave. I'm going to explain one time and one time only. This is a rest leave and that is what I intend to make it. I never doubt a thing you do, so please do the same with your hubby.... I only intend to take $40 with me and will probably spend $30 on stuff for you. I'm probably a big flop as far as a husband goes but I try hard to do right. Really I do. After the statement I made (probably telling her she could date one guy while he was gone) I probably have little right to eat you out I'll be damned if I will have you drinking with (a male friend), that stuff's got to come to a screaming halt, have fun sweet, but leave the mixed drinks out."

He then said he was flying 150 hours a week, adding, "I'm beginning to believe that crash at Pecos did more than hurt my jaw. I'm getting worse by the day at forgetting things. I guess it's just the strain of so much flying, but I guess it will turn out alright."

1/24/45

"Hardly a night passes I don't dream of you. Sometimes they are so real I almost believe this is all a dream and I will wake up and find you in my arms."

Then he tried again to explain why he wanted to take his leave in Australia instead of taking an extremely fast and short trip home:

"I can see why you are so curious about these Sidney leaves cause there are some tall tales about those leaves. Don't let it worry you cause no place will ever compare to (a U.S. airbase where he was stationed) and I wasn't ruined there."

1/25/45

A short note from Charlie says he is "moving again." He doesn't say where, but he adds that he is flying so much that he expects "I will get a medal before long."

1/27/45

Ruth learned that he now was somewhere in the Philippines. Charlie said he had the last of his clothes and is living for a while in a pup tent.

"I am flying regular combat missions and living in the field." Unfortunately he said "2 buddies didn't show up" among those returning from a mission. Strangely, Charlie says he is "supposed to go home in a couple of weeks." Going home wouldn't occur for many months.

1/28/45

Charlie said he had two sets of Khakis now and he and a friend were living in a tent on the beach (that's also right next to a Philippine village). "We take showers in the open and girls come by each night to watch."

3/10/45

Charlie tells Ruth he will be leaving the squadron for special training. He didn't explain what type of training. He added that "some of the boys are getting drunk after they found out that they are not going home." He added, "I'll be home by X-mas."

3/24/45

Japanese planes bombed the air base late the previous night. Charlie was in his airplane.

"I jumped out of the plane—a good 15 feet—and made a dash for a dugout." He said he ran over the crew chief and landed in a large puddle of water. "I've never been so wet, muddy and cold ever."

3/27/45

Charlie reported to Ruth that he has been hospitalized for the last two days due to "a good case of Flier's Fatigue or better yet Pilot's Nerves."Three days later he wrote a short note with one positive thing: "There's good food at the hospital."

About this time, Charlie was grounded because of his fatigue and nerve problems. He couldn't fly as a pilot again until he was cleared after a hearing. As readers will see in later letters, the issue bothered him. but he tried to make the best of it by contributing to work on projects on the ground.

3/31/45

He reported that he was underweight and his nerves were shot. But, he claimed, that his fellow members of the 69th TC Squadron "treat me like a king. We had a party at the house all night." Referring to me, he asks Ruth, "Is little bud of mine still as mean as ever?" And he recommended a movie called "Winged Victory," a 1944 musical war picture.

April,1945 was a rather confusing time for Charlie on the question of whether he was flying or was grounded. On April 6 he told Ruth in a letter that he was supposed to start flying again. He said he needed "a check ride" to make sure his nerve problem was in check. On April 12 he wrote that he needed to get his story up to date. He told Ruth that her "ol' puddle foot hubby" was working hard at the Officers Club but he took a check ride "and made two beautiful landings." But the grounding stayed in effect.

4/13/45

News had come that President Franklin Roosevelt had died the previous day. Charlie wrote Ruth that it was "the death of a great man."

5/19/45

Charlie confessed that he was "down in the dumps." It bothered him that he had been officially grounded. He told Ruth that he hoped he could keep his silver wings. In his next several letters he strained to make his grounded life sound interesting, such as "I played craps and won" and he listened to interesting things on his radio. But occasionally it slipped out that "I hope to fly again."

5/19/45

Finally, the Chief Officer offered hope that he could again be flying: "The CO told me I am just temporarily grounded," he told Ruth. Also, he learned that he wouldn't have to go before an approval board before winning the right to fly again. "I'm so well liked in the squadron (the CO) asked to keep me in the 69th (Squadron)." Charlie said he hoped that with all the good war news out of Europe "people remember there's a war still going on over here."

The war in Europe officially ended on May 8, 1945, with the suicide of Adolph Hitler and unconditional surrender of Germany. The war with Japan would not be over officially until the signing of surrender documents aboard the USS Missouri on September 2, 1945.

5/23/45

Charlie's squadron had moved to "somewhere in the Philippines," where he wrote Ruth about the joy of drinking beer. "I used to not like beer, but I'm enjoying it more now."

5/30/45

Charlie was upset. Ruth had written him that our mother and a neighbor had been "talking" about her. We don't know the details, but apparently it was unpleasant, and Ruth somehow learned about it. "I read your letter about people talking about you," he wrote to Ruth. He said he had written to mom and the neighbor "expressing my desire that they mind their own business." But he also told Ruth: "'I'm so nervous don't tell me what people say. It will take a long time to get over it."

6/9/45

From the Philippines, Charlie wrote a strange letter. He said he was still a pilot but grounded. He then explained that he had missed three days of writing after he was shot in his right arm: "not a serious injury but makes it hard to write." He didn't explain how he can still be a pilot while grounded or shot in the arm while grounded at his base.

6/13/45

Charlie had a cold, but was staying busy on squadron business. "I'm still a pilot as far as the squadron is concerned," he wrote. He saw the movie "Tonight and Every Night," a 1945 musical starring Rita Hayworth.

6/16/45

Charlie said he still is waiting for pictures of Ruth in a grass skirt; otherwise, life is the same old day after day." He added that he "can't seem to think straight."

6/24/45

Charlie told Ruth that he had flown for the first time in a long time, "Nick let me take the controls." He added: "I've been a husband for one year."

6/25/45

Charlie told Ruth that in the Philippines he spends most of his time at the beach. He closed with: "It's hard to realize that we've been married one year."

6/29/45

Charlie and most of the squadron moved to a different base on Luzon, the Philippines. His friend Hank stayed behind to take down their shack. Hank had promised that he would send flowers to Ruth for the anniversary.

7/1/45

"Somewhere on Luzon. I really do like it here," he wrote. "It's much cooler and the people are really nice."

Residents of a nearby town put on a stage show for the soldiers. Charlie said he planned to start work on a residential shack for him and friends the next day.

7/2/45

Manila, the capital of the Philippines, was close enough to the new base that Charlie visited it several times, particularly to buy gifts for Ruth. He was impressed by the food. He also had worked on the shack, but he said it wouldn't be as nice as the one they left at the previous base.

8/3/45

"I got my Austin High diploma," he told Ruth. "I plan to enter the university when I get back."

And he did just that. He and Ruth lived in married student housing, and he earned a degree in geology, becoming the first university graduate in our family. I became the second one, earning a Bachelor of Journalism in 1963 and a Bachelor of Arts with a dual major in Government and English in 1964. Unfortunately, as you will learn later, Charlie was no longer living at that time. My daughter,

Rachel Davis, earned a third from Southwestern University at Georgetown, Texas, with a double major in English and Women's Studies in 1995. She did much of the research and editing on this book.

8/6/45

At Clarks Field on Luzon, Charlie wrote that he is packed and ready to leave for home in a week. He told Ruth about four of the base's pilots, thinking in error that the war was over, taking a plane and flying to Japan. He said they landed at a Japanese military airfield and took a train to Tokyo. They were surprised when they didn't see any U.S. troops in the city, so they took the train back to their plane and flew back to their base. V-J Day was August 14, 1945. It is unclear if something like that really happened or was just a rumor.

8/8/45

He was elated to have received nine letters at one time from Ruth and others. He also was happy to write that the war was almost over. He described going to Okinawa, the site of a major battle a few months earlier. "I didn't like it," he said without telling why.

8/9/45

Charlie told Ruth that he had been listening to newscasts about the war. "It's really swell that Russia decided to come in. The atomic bomb has really caused a lot of excitement around here. It's almost like something Buck Rogers would use in the funny paper, If the war is over this year I'll be home by spring."

8/12/45

"All hell broke loose," Charlie told Ruth. "All the guns started shooting and parachute flares went off everywhere. Someone shouted It's a jap raid. We dived for our guns then we heard over the radio peace terms had been sent to the allies. We almost tore the place down, whiskey and Cokes came out."

8/13/45

"We heard we accepted the peace terms. I can hardly realize it all, I wish you could have seen us boil when we heard a report that the people back home didn't want to accept the offer, I can hardly believe our own people would do that, ... The Squadron has a new name: Front Line Airlines, ... If the war ends we could be home by X-mas or spring."

8/15/45

"One million prayers have been answered on this day, I just heard the news this war is over, went down to the Mess Hall and told them to fix the best meal they could for this happens to be a great day for all, I kept the Mess Hall open all night–120 gallons of coffee."

After Charlie was grounded, managing the Mess Hall was one of his duties.

8/20/45

On Luzon, Charlie wrote that he hasn't received any mail for two weeks. "I can't realize the world is at peace again, for we do the same ol' thing day after day, sometimes I catch myself saying, 'I'll be glad when the war is over" Before he heads home, he says, "I hope to take in the sights in Japan."

8/22/45

"I can't write each day," he told Ruth, "Now that the war is over Troop Carrier has just begun to start work, We are hoping to be among the first to reach Japan but it seems the WACs always beat us."

The Women's Army Corps was a division of the U.S. Army created during World War II.

8/25/45

Charlie wrote Ruth that he admits he "piddled around" in their relationship, but he adds: "I loved you since our first date." He also admitted: "The last years have left me with a bad case of nerves." And ends with "Love and kisses Charles." Rather than his usual "Love Chas."

8/29/45

"Been listening to the latest news, seems that our boys will land in Japan without any trouble." He wrote. He also has learned that his squadron at some point will go to Japan as part of the occupation forces. "I always wanted to see Japan and I guess I will get my wish."

9/12/45

Charlie told Ruth that his stay with his squadron "will be a little longer" than he thought but he "should be home in October. ... "I'll get a promotion when I get to the states, probably get to a hospital again to do something about my nerves."

9/16/45

"Still at Luzon, still expecting to leave, but lots of confusion "all the cooks have gone home & the Mess Hall has shut down," he said. "I just want to go home." A few days later he told her it looks like it will be "a little later than I said. The squadron is in Japan and I might need to go there to get my orders." Three days later he told her that he went to Manilla (the Philippine's capital) to check on getting orders to go home, and added that now he'll be home "the middle of November at the earliest."

10/01/45

Tachikawa Field, Tokyo, Japan.

"Dear Ruth. I'm sure the address is a surprise, I left Luzon & flew to Okanspat, gassed up and flew to Koniya Naval Air Base to spend the night, visited the town if you can call what was left a town, flew a round-about way to see 2 places where atomic bombs fell, first one was torn up," he wrote. He said the second place gave him "the most creepy feeling a person ever had for the site was the most God forsaken site on this earth, where a once beautiful city stood at the ocean's edge there was not a thing left, the whole town was as flat as the palm of your hand, we flew real low and could see only a handful of people." His letter said they were living in a hangar at the air base. The Japanese army "sends 200 soldiers out each day for us to use as we see fit," adding that the Japanese people are extremely friendly and helpful. Charlie's description of the flight in his letter to Ruth made it sound like he was flying the airplane, but there was no indication that his grounding had been lifted.

10/4/45

"It's really cold here," Charlie complained to Ruth from Japan, adding that he sleeps under two Army blankets. Their water comes from a mountain stream. "It's like taking a bath in ice water." He described how they went through some caves and discovered tools and airplane parts.

10/5/45

Charlie told Ruth that a member of his group was sent home based on the same number of points that he had, adding "I haven't the slightest idea what happened."

10/7/45

He reported the good news that he has 82 points, the highest number in his squadron, which should put him first in line to return to the states. This letter describes how the other members of the squadron bought a geisha house for the night. He adds: "None of the girls can speak English but these guys can get what they want in any language."

10/10/45

A self-described "Man of Leisure," Charlie acquired a jeep for himself and three friends to visit a small town in the mountains north of Tokyo. He described the reaction of the town's children to their visit: "I got a kick out of it. It reminds a person of some little dog that had received his first look at a tree. They just went wild. Kids stand at the side of the road and wave and say, 'Hi Joe' just like our kids would do." Charlie piled a bunch of kids into the back of the jeep and took them for a ride.

10/18/45

"The glad day has arrived for I received my orders to come home," he exclaimed in a letter to Ruth. He said he first had to find a plane ride to go back to Manilla to process the paperwork and arrange a final plane ride to the States. He said if everything goes well he'd be home by Thanksgiving. "I spent the day with 'Brass Hats' trying to leave from Japan but red tape had me behind the 8 ball from the very start."

10/25/45

He got on a plane headed for Manilla, but it had engine trouble and couldn't go. But that turned out to be a blessing for Charlie, because when the troubled plane got back to Japan he found new orders letting him leave for the U.S. from Japan. While waiting for his flight to the States, he and a buddy checked out a jeep and saw the sights around Tokyo and Yokohama. He closed the letter to Ruth with: "I miss you so much I can hardly wait to see you."

10/28/45

Charlie writes that he is "tired, sleepy and dirty. I took a trip to the small town of Ome in search of some gifts, went to a house and got some swell shots of children in their colorful robes.... We have an issue of 5 bottles of Jap beer a week, I like Jap beer so much better than stateside."

10/29/45

Tachikawa Japan.

"This has really been a nice day," he wrote, with chicken for lunch and steak for dinner and then a Japanese stage show that night. "My roommate and I left a little early and were trying to find our way out of the building when we opened the wrong door, it happen(ed) to be the room the Jap girls were using, you may quote me as saying the Jap girls have very nice shapes."

CHARLIE GOES HOME

That analysis of the figures of Japanese women was Charlie's last letter to Ruth. Soon he was on his way home. And after he got back to join Ruth, of course, there was no need for letters. He enrolled at the University of Texas under the G.I. Bill that helped pay his expenses, and he and Ruth lived in married student housing. His nerves still bothered him, and a doctor told him to relax and do something he enjoyed. For Charlie, that was fishing. He bought an Army Surplus rubber raft, constructed a wooden platform for the rear and purchased a one-half horse-power outboard motor to go on the platform. He frequently would pick me up and take me fishing in the raft.

After four years he became the first member of our family to graduate from college, receiving a degree in geology that ultimately led to a career in the oil and gas industry. But that was delayed because he had remained in the Air Force Reserve and was called up for active duty in the early 1950s during the Korean War. He and Ruth moved to Tucson, Arizona, where he had a desk job at an Air Force base and Ruth gave birth to their son Donald in 1952.

Ruth with baby Donnie in Arizona, 1952.

The family moved several times after the Korean War ended, and Charlie began his career in the oil and gas industry. They ultimately settled in Oklahoma City with Charlie working for an oil company. There, tragedy struck in 1961. Charlie was attending a meeting in a downtown office building. When the meeting was over, he left with two other company employees, riding in the back seat of the car. At that time, seatbelts were required only for front seats. According to what the authorities told the family, as the driver was pulling out of the parking garage his car was struck by a stolen car driven by a fifteen-year-old boy being chased by the police. Without a seatbelt, Charlie was thrown out of the car and run over by another car. He died at a hospital.

Ruth then took their young son Donald and moved to College Station, Texas, where her sister Helen lived with her husband, Al Price, and their children. Al was a professor at Texas A&M University. Ruth got a job with the Texas Transportation Institute at the university. She was serving as the institute's executive secretary when she died of cancer at a local hospital in 1979. She was 58.

Ruth with her young niece Becky Bachschmid while visiting family.

Donald Davis began a successful career in radio at a local station. That led to an on-the-air position in Virginia and then to one in the American Virgin Islands. Unfortunately, a hurricane struck the area while he was there. Donald was walking along a flooded street trying to check on the station when some armed looters began shooting at him. He dove into a ditch filled with filthy water. He escaped the looters but something in the water got into his bloodstream and attacked his heart. Knowing something was wrong, he flew back to Virginia and immediately underwent a heart operation. After about a year of recuperating, he again began announcing at a Virginia radio station. He became sick while on the air and died on the way to a hospital. He was 39.

Charlie and Ruth are buried together with a single marker at Memorial Park Cemetery in Austin. Donald is buried nearby.

THE DAILY OKLAHOMAN Thursday, April 13, 1961 3

Crash Victim's Rites Pending

Services for Charles Edwin Davis, 38, of 2724 Clermont Pl., who died Wednesday from injuries suffered Tuesday in an auto accident at NW 3 and Lee, are pending at Sherman Funeral Home.

Davis, a senior geophysicist with Pan American Petroleum Corp., had lived in the city since 1956. He came here from Jackson, Miss.

Born in Grand Prairie, Texas, Davis was schooled in Austin and was graduated from high school there in 1941. He received his BA in geology from the University of Texas in 1950 and attended graduate school there.

Davis served in the U. S. Air Force during World War II and the Korean War. He was discharged as first lieutenant in 1953 and until his death was a captain in the inactive reserve.

He was a member and deacon of Greystone Presbyterian Church.

Surviving are his wife, Ruth, and son Donald, both of the home; his mother, Mrs. Ross Davis, and a brother, James L. Davis, both of Austin, Texas.

CONTRIBUTORS

Becky Bachschmid of Fort Worth, Texas, a niece of Ruth and friend of her and Donald Davis who contributed information and loaned a series of photographs to us.

Byron Bachschmid of Midland, Texas, brother of Becky who also contributed information and loaned photographs. Ruth was an aunt to both Becky and Byron.

Nancy Hopkins Reily of West Lake Hills, Texas, author of several published books, including two on Georgia O'Keeffe, who gave us advise on writing and publishing.

Linda and Don Shafer of Austin Texas, longtime friends who helped with editing and proofreading. They are editors-in-chief for an international engineering society and co-authors of Software Engineering courses and publications, including four books.

Ruth Davis - Charlie's love

Back home for Christmas

www.ingramcontent.com/pod-product-compliance
Lightning Source LLC
LaVergne TN
LVHW050610100826
845148LV00015B/3204

9781632937865